From Darkness to Light

Christina Hollander

BookLeaf Publishing

India | USA | UK

Presentation by *BookLeaf Publishing*

Web: www.bookleafpub.com

E-mail: info@bookleafpub.com

ISBN: 9789357447768

First edition 2021

To my daddy who was also born a writer and
died too early

ACKNOWLEDGEMENT

Thanks to my family for always being there for
me and for always supporting me
Thanks to my friends who have always believed
in me
Thanks to my mental health community for
never leaving me alone
I love you all so much

PREFACE

I have always wanted to write a book. I have been suffering from depression and anxiety since many years. It is a never ending battle. I am blessed for all the love I get from my family and friends. I was born a writer. I have my own blog and gave a speech at the United Nations in 2015. With this book I want to help and inspire others. Writing is healing. I hope you all will feel less alone when you are reading my book. The poems will be mental health related.

The universe

The universe is big
So big
What am I doing here? Why do I think about
this question all the time? What is my purpose?
It makes me feel anxious, depressed, but also
hopeful
Our problems aren't that important
But why do we keep thinking about them all the
time instead of living our lives to the fullest?
Having a mental illness is horrible
What makes it only a bit better
Is to watch the stars and the moon
It makes me feel a bit hopeful
If only for a bit
For a while I feel at peace
I am alive
Surviving
And that's it

World Mental Health Day

I close my eyes
All I see and feel is darkness
I feel lost
I'm not myself anymore
My chest feels tight
I'm breathing faster
My heart rate is racing
So many thoughts about the future
I'm nauseous
I'm getting dizzy
Cold
Warm
I'm getting crazy
Why can't I just feel like a normal person?
I begin to cry
What's happening to me?

This is what it feels to suffer from anxiety and
panic attacks
It's the worst
1 of 5 people suffer on a daily basis with their
mental health
Depression, bipolar, borderline, eating disorder,
psychoses, anxiety, ocd
Any person can suffer from one or more of them
They all matter

No matter your nationality, gender, age, race
Mental illnesses are real
There's no need to shame
What we need is compassion, support and respect
A better mental health system
Every illness counts
Time is ticking
It's time to save lives
Change the mental health care system
We don't want more deaths
We want better treatments available for all
Because
We all deserve to feel safe, loved and get the help we need whenever we need it
Our time is now
Let's all fight for a better system and society
We are not alone
We are all in this together always 
We are warriors
Love you all
Amen

Suffering from anxiety

Suffering from anxiety is being anxious but still smiling

Suffering from anxiety means crying

Suffering from anxiety is feeling nauseous

Suffering from anxiety is having constant worries

Suffering from anxiety is overthinking all the time

Suffering from anxiety is feeling dizzy

Suffering from anxiety is being afraid to die during a panic attack

Suffering from anxiety is being afraid to leave your home

Suffering from anxiety is cancelling plans with your friends

Suffering from anxiety is not knowing what is wrong

Suffering from anxiety is constant living
between escaping your fears or facing them and
feeling anxious

Suffering from anxiety is being tired of feeling
anxious all the time

Suffering from anxiety is a hell

Suffering from anxiety is being afraid of
searching for a job or going to school

Suffering from anxiety is being afraid of doing
daily things

Suffering from anxiety means feeling your heart
beating fast

Suffering from anxiety is hard because it's an
invisible mental illness

Suffering from anxiety is not something you
choose

Suffering from anxiety is an illness which you
have to fight every day with

Endless battle

Sometimes it all feels like an endless battle
When will these racing thoughts go away?
When will I feel okay again?
I just want a sign
To keep going on
That is all I need

Life is hard

They say he has died
It isn't true
My daddy lives
I don't believe it
This is insane
I can't deal with it
Loss
Grief
What's going on?
How can I survive without you?
I have no idea
Please daddy come back to me
I want to hug you hard
And never let you go
I can't sleep
I can't eat
Depression is coming back like never before
I want to escape forever
Life makes no sense

Life is a mystery

Life is strange
One day your loved one is there
And the next day
He dies
And
Suddenly you feel alone
In this big world
Without a clue at all

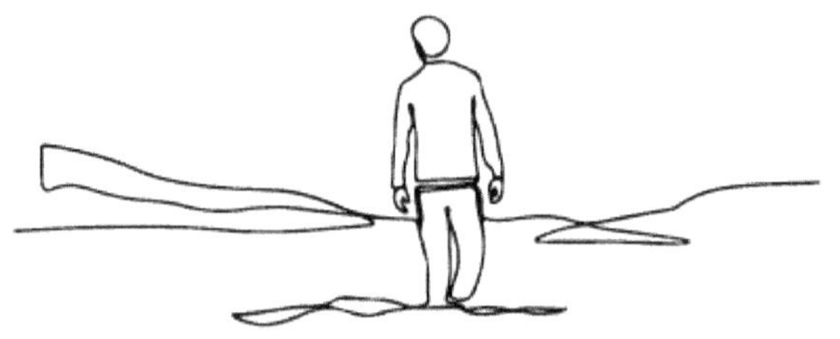

My mind is a battlefield

I have racing thoughts
They never stop
Only when I sleep
At that moment
I can finally be at peace
Even if it is
For one moment

When will this suffering end?

Will I ever feel happy?
Will my suffering ever end?
When will I feel normal?
Nobody knows the answer
I just wish
That one day
I will be happy
And live a life worth living

Purpose of life

The purpose of life is feeling the roller coaster
emotions going up and down
That makes you feel alive

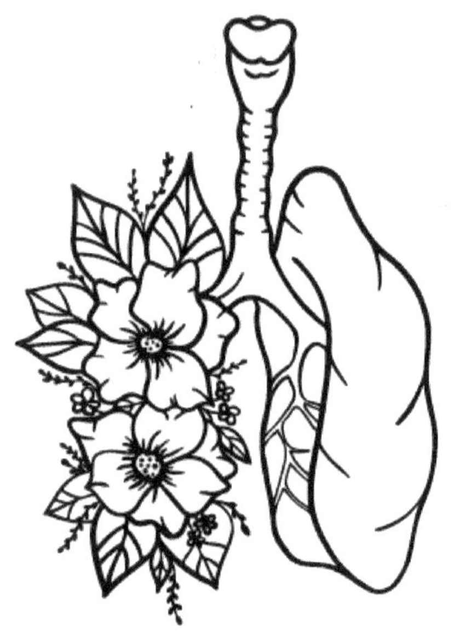

Feeling alive

I hear the wind blowing
I see the waves coming
I taste the salty sea
I smell the salty air
And for one moment
I feel alive
Surfing is freedom
And
The sea
Is my home

My heart

My heart is an ocean of emotions and memories
It is full of light and darkness
It all belongs there
You can't have only light
Or darkness
Your heart is made for it all
Feeling emotions is what makes you feel alive

The sun and the moon

The sun makes you happy
And the moon lets you feel

The moon and I

I'm looking at the moon
I see her shining brightly in the dark sky
She makes me feel less alone
She's telling me to shine too
She whispers: "You can shine in the dark times"
You can go through it
If I can do it
You can do it too
Remember, if you ever feel lonely look up at the
sky
I'm right there
You are never alone 🤍

Sweet life

Life is like a flower
We grow old
And die
Life is short
But
Beautiful

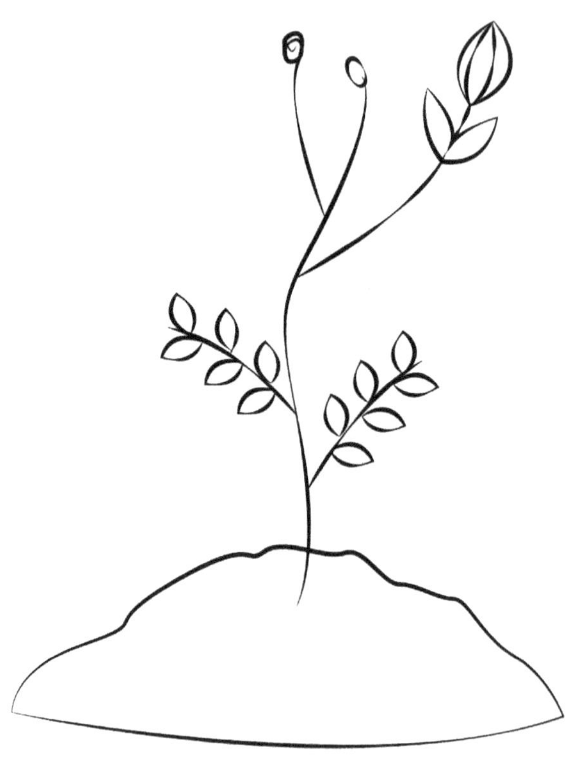

Wild nature

I'm a wild flower
I grow in the most beautiful places
I'm different than the other flowers
It makes me unique
I'm free and wild as nature

That's what real love is

She is vulnerable and sensitive
She is funny but oh so fragile
She is wild and crazy
She is beautiful and smart
She is romantic and creative
She is all you ever wanted
But
She is also the girl who cries herself to sleep
She can feel sad for no reason
She get anxious very fast
She has mood swings
She is sometimes hard to deal with
If you really want to love her you will have to
love every part of her because that's what love is
about
Accepting the person for who they are and
loving them unconditionally
Then you know it's real love 💔

Power in the midst of chaos

In the midst of chaos I found power
Power in myself that I haven't felt for a long
time
I'm so much stronger than I think
If I can face loss and grief
Then I can and will achieve all my dreams
One step at a time
For me and for my daddy
I will make it true

Never give up

We all need to know that we will find a light
through our darkest times

We all need to know that we can go through hard
times in life

We all need to know that feelings come and go

We all need to know that life is about the little
moments

We all need to know that better things are
coming

We all need to know that life's about finding the
balance between the good and the bad

We all need to know that life's hard but we are
tougher

We all need to know that we are loved

We all need to know that we aren't alone in our
feelings and thoughts

We all need to know that there's someone who feels exactly the same way as we do

We all need to know that this too shall pass

We all need to know that we will find a purpose in life

We all need to know that being alive is the greatest gift of all

We all need to know that true happiness is loving yourself unconditionally

We all need to know that there will be a time where we find our happiness again

We all need to know that we are warriors and that we won't give up

We all need to know that we are all in this together and that we will stick together

Keep going lovelies, never give up!

I am good enough

I am sensitive

I am caring

I am beautiful

I am creative

I am inspiring

I am strong

I am lovable

I am enough

I am loved

I am empathetic

I am vulnerable

I am honest

I am open-minded

I am intelligent

I am sweet

I am romantic

I can be all of them

I don't have to choose between one of them

Being human means being all of those things

That's the power of being human

To be who you want to be without having to choose

Being ourselves and loving ourselves unconditionally

We are all human and matter

Be yourself and love yourself

Just be you

Internet friends

I don't see you but I know you are there
We are separated by land or sea
We connect through the internet
Lots of miles are between us
How beautiful is it that even though we have
never met
I can feel such a beautiful friendship
Each day our friendship grows and grows
The universe connected us
We will always be there for each other
I know one day will come that we will finally
see each other
Nothing will change between us
I will hug you and tell you how much I love you
Our friendship will be forever
Thank you for being such a good friend 🩶